THE ROYAL NAVY IN FOCUS 1920-29

Compiled by Lt. Cdr. Ben Warlow RN

£7.95

Editor's Note

This is the sixth volume of the Royal Navy in Focus series and again the photographs are from the archives of Wright and Logan. Over the years they have been mainly concerned with the Portsmouth and Portland naval scene, but have also broadened their horizons by taking over the negatives from A & J Pavia at Malta, and this book contains a fair sample of both home pictures and those taken in the sunnier climes of Malta.

These photographs have been assembled to cover the Royal Navy of the Twenties, a period when the maritime air aspects were covered by the Royal Air Force, and because of that, some photographs are included which would appear to belong to that service. However, as they were only acting "in loco parentis", it seemed right to include them to provide a fully balanced view of the maritime defence of that period.

Despite many of these vessels having been built during or even before the First World War, it is surprising to see how many went on to endure the Second World War. Old ships were very valuable and worth their weight in gold in 1939, and some were even brought back from the shadow of the breaker's yard. It is perhaps a sobering thought that even with the large Fleet that we had in September 1939, we were stretched to the limit to support Britain's food and oil supplies against a relatively smaller enemy. A look at today's Navy, seventy years on, may make that an even more worrying reflection . . .

Mike Critchley,
Liskeard,
Cornwall.

HMS ADVENTURE (1928)

The ADVENTURE was the first surface warship laid down after the signing of peace. Built at Devonport Dockyard, she was commissioned for trials in April 1927 and then for the Atlantic Fleet a month later to replace the converted liner PRINCESS MARGARET. Despite being of 6740 tons, her main defensive armament was only four single 4.7 inch AA guns. She could carry over 300 mines and had diesel electric engines for cruising. She is seen here at Portland, under the command of Captain J H D Cunningham MVO, in her original guise. In 1931 she was paid off and her square stern was made round. She served on the China Station from 1933-38, with just 6 days at home in June 1936 to recommission. At the outbreak of war she helped lay a mine barrage in the Dover Strait. She was twice damaged by mines and once by a collision. She was used to transport mines to Russia and depth charges to the Mediterranean. In 1944 she became a repair ship and was broken up in 1947.

HMS AMBROSE (May 1928)

The AMBROSE had been built by Raylton Dixon of Middlesborough for the Booth Line, but was hired on 10 December 1914 and fitted out as an Armed Merchant Cruiser. In March 1915 she was attacked three times by a submarine in the North Channel, all the torpedoes missed and the submarine disappeared after AMBROSE fired at her. She was purchased in October 1915 and converted to a submarine depot ship and is seen here returning from China where she had, with TITANIA and MARAZION, supported the Fourth Flotilla. In June 1938 she was renamed COCHRANE and became the depot at Rosyth, being sold in August 1946.

HMS ASSISTANCE (October 1927)

The ASSISTANCE was a 9600 ton repair ship, purchased in September 1900 and launched by Raylton Dixon 3 months later. She is seen here returning from a cruise to Ajaccio, Genoa, Messina and Naples. She remained on the Mediterranean Station until January 1930, when she was relieved by the RESOURCE, which had just been completed at Barrow. She was then placed in reserve and was handed over to Wards, in March 1937, in part payment for the MAJESTIC.

HMAS AUSTRALIA (1928)

The AUSTRALIA commissioned on the Clyde on 24 April 1928. One of the first group of the COUNTY Class, her external bulges are seen catching the overhead Sun here, whilst her quadruple torpedo tubes amidships are trained outboard and are casting a shadow. After trials, she and the CANBERRA had their funnels raised by 18 feet, 3 feet more than the RN members of the class. She is flying the flag of Rear Admiral G F Hyde CVO CBE, Commanding HM Australian Squadron. The aircraft catapult abaft her funnels was not completed until 1935. After a fortnight at Portland, she left Spithead at midnight 2/3 August for Australia via Canada, the Panama Canal and New Zealand. She served throughout World War II, being damaged by kamikaze aircraft. Repaired, she served until 1954 and was broken up in 1955, some parts of her being incorporated in the damage control training units at HMAS PENGUIN, Sydney.

HMS BARHAM (May 1929)

The BARHAM was a QUEEN ELIZABETH Class battleship completed by Clydebank in October 1915. She was the Flagship of the Fifth Battle Squadron at Jutland and was hit by 6 heavy shells losing 26 dead and 37 wounded. She is seen here arriving at Malta from Villefranche and about to transfer the Flag of the First Battle Squadron to the REVENGE. She was the last of the class to receive her large refit when her funnels were trunked together and bulges were fitted. This refit took place in 1930-33, when she was also given a tripod mainmast and a McTaggart catapult on X turret. She never received a second major modernisation. In December 1939 she rammed and sank the destroyer DUCHESS, and later was torpedoed by U30. After repairs she went to the Mediterranean, was at Matapan and was damaged off Crete. On 25 November 1941 she was hit by 4 torpedoes from U331 off Sollum, capsized and blew up in 5 minutes. 862 officers and men were lost.

HMS BENBOW (July 1928)

The BENBOW was an IRON DUKE Class battleship of 25,000 tons, launched by Beardmore on 12 November 1913. These ships introduced 6 inch secondary armaments and were the last coal burning battleships. They were "wet ships", the after 6 inch guns being removed as they could not be operated in a seaway, and Q and Y turrets were difficult to man in rough weather. She was Flagship of the Second Battle Squadron at Jutland, and took part in Black Sea operations after the war. She is seen here after recommissioning (with the crew of the IRON DUKE) as Flagship of the Third Battle Squadron. She paid off in 1929 and was sold in March 1931.

HMS BLACKWATER (1929)

Launched as the WILLIAM INWOOD by Cochrane in 1918, she was renamed BLACKWATER in 1920. A MERSEY Type trawler of 438 tons standard, she had been transferred from Portsmouth to Portland in 1927 to work for the Anti-Submarine School in HMS OSPREY as a tender to HMS HEATHER. For this task she was disarmed and had a deckhouse fitted abaft the funnel. In 1939 she was fitted as a minesweeper—with a LL sweep—at Leith and then worked off the East Coast during the war. In 1945 she was based on Ostend and finally paid off in February 1946 before being sold for commercial service.

HMS BOYNE (1929)

A MERSEY Type trawler built by Cochrane as the WILLIAM JONES in 1918, she was renamed in 1920. She replaced the GARRY on Fishery Protection duties in 1924 and in 1926 became one of the two trawlers used to train the RNR in minesweeping, operating from Portland. At the end of 1928 she returned to Fishery Protection duties and is seen here in that role, armed and with her crew fallen in smartly. For most of 1929 she operated off the East Coast as the "headquarters" of Local Fishery Officer, North Sea, with visits to Norway and Scotland. She was sold in 1946 and renamed NYPUBERG.

HMS BROKE (1929)

A Thornycroft built destroyer leader of the SHAKESPEARE Class, the BROKE had been launched as the ROOKE on 16 September 1920, but was renamed on 13 April 1921. She was completed at Pembroke Dock in January 1925. Built to lead V and W Class destroyers, she became the leader of the Fourth Mediterranean Flotilla until 1931. The BROKE was attached to RNEC Keyham from 1931. In June 1940 she withdrew the demolition parties from Brest and that October went to aid the damaged liner EMPRESS OF BRITAIN. In April 1941 she rescued the crew of the burning AMC CORMORIN. Later that summer she was in collision with the destroyer VERITY. In November 1942 she attacked the harbour at Algiers with parties embarked to prevent French ships scuttling and the demolition of port facilities. She entered at the fourth attempt, landed her parties and then withdrew, sinking the next day.

HMS CACHALOT (20 July 1929)

The CACHALOT was one of 15 Z Class Admiralty Whalers built in 1915. Originally called Z7, she was launched by Smith's Dock on 28 July 1915. Of 336 tons, she originally carried a 12 pounder gun. After the war she reduced to a reserve complement at Portland and then became part of the Anti-Submarine Flotilla working from that Base. She was paid off on 31 August 1932 and was sold in 1933, being renamed GLADIATOR.

HMS CAIRO (July 1929)

The CAIRO was in the last group of the C class cruisers, being launched on the Clyde on 19 November 1918. She was completed with a trawl bow which made a further improvement to her weatherliness. Here she is seen leaving Malta for Greek waters flying the Flag of the Rear Admiral Commanding Destroyer Flotillas in the Mediterranean, in charge of 4 Leaders and 32 destroyers. She was converted to an AA ship at Chatham in 1939, having a multiple pom pom in B position, and twin 4 inch guns in place of the other four 6 inch guns. She was damaged by bombs in the Norwegian campaign and during Operation Pedestal in August 1942 was torpedoed by the Italian submarine AXUM and had to be sunk by other RN ships.

HMS CALEDON (November 1927)

The CALEDON was launched by Cammell Laird on 25 November 1916. This class introduced the straight bow to the C classes, and they were built with only two shafts. They were also fitted with two pairs of torpedo tubes each side on the upper deck amidships. CALEDON is seen here entering Malta having commissioned at the Nore in September for the Third Cruiser Squadron in the Mediterranean. She has a "flying off platform" fitted abaft her funnels. Shortly afterwards she damaged her bow in a collision with an Italian oiler in the Doro Channel and had to be towed back to Malta—stern first. In 1942/3 she was converted for anti-aircraft work, her bridge being moved aft and twin 4 inch guns fitted in A, B and Y positions. She then served in the Mediterranean, was placed in reserve in 1945 and sold in 1948.

HMS CALYPSO (February 1927)

The CALEDON Class cruiser CALYPSO is seen here passing the aircraft carrier EAGLE as she enters Grand Harbour. She had been launched by Hawthorn Leslie on 24 January 1917 and when completed joined the Grand Fleet. She was hit by a shell from a German cruiser during the Battle of Heligoland Bight in November, 1917, everyone in her conning tower being killed. She served in the Baltic in 1918-9 prior to joining the Mediterranean Fleet, where she remained, apart from refits, until 1932. She returned to the Mediterranean during the Second World War. She was torpedoed by the Italian Submarine ALPINO BAGNOLINI South of Crete on 12 June 1940 with the loss of 39 men.

HMS CAMBRIAN (1927)

The CAMBRIAN was the nameship of the third group of C Class cruisers. Designed to be armed with two 6 inch and eight 4 inch guns, her forecastle pair of 4 inch were replaced by a 6 inch before she joined the Fleet in May 1916—a fourth 6 inch was fitted later. By the end of the war her pole foremast had been replaced by a tripod, and soon after a searchlight control position amidships was removed to lessen topweight and reduce rolling. She is seen here when part of the Second Cruiser Squadron of the Atlantic Fleet. In the spring she had been to Oran and the summer was spent in the North Sea and visiting Scandanavia. After a period trooping in 1929 she went into reserve. She was sold in July 1934.

HMS CAMPBELL (July 1929)

An Admiralty Type destroyer leader, CAMPBELL was launched by Cammell Laird on 21 September 1918. She carried five 4.7 inch guns, (the fifth mounted between her funnels), a single 4 inch abaft the after funnel and two triple sets of torpedo tubes. She is seen here when leader of the 6th Flotilla of the Atlantic Fleet, commanded by Captain T S V Phillips, later to lose his life when the PRINCE OF WALES was sunk in December 1941. The CAMPBELL was converted to a short range escort in the Second World War, and took part in the attack on the SCHARNHORST, GNEISENAU and PRINZ EUGEN as they steamed up the Channel in February 1942. She was broken up in June 1948.

HMAS CANBERRA (1928)

The CANBERRA was launched on Clydebank on 31 May 1927, the same month as her name city was inaugurated by The Duke of York. Commissioned on the Clyde on 9 July 1928, she then sailed for Portsmouth where she and her sister, the AUSTRALIA, were visited by H M King George. After trials, she sailed for Australia. In the 1930s her catapult fitting was completed and her AA gunnery arrangements were improved. In March 41 she and the LEANDER caught the supply ships COBURG and KETTY BROVIG. In July 42 she joined the screening force for the amphibious squadron for the Solomons. On the night 8/9 August a Japanese cruiser force attacked the force off Savo Island. The CANBERRA was hit by two torpedoes and many shells and had to be sunk the next morning. The Americans later named a cruiser in her honour.

HMS CANTERBURY (1928)

CANTERBURY was one of four ships of the CAMBRIAN Class, built with two single 6 inch and eight single 4 inch guns, but re-armed as the CAROLINE Class had been with four 6 inch and two 3 inch AA guns. Launched on the Clyde on 21 December 1915, she served in the Harwich force during the war and then in the Aegean and Black Sea before becoming a gunnery training ship at Portsmouth in 1919. After a spell in reserve she served with the Atlantic Fleet in the Second Cruiser Squadron from 1924 to 1930 before being placed in reserve at the Nore. She undertook several trooping trips before being sold in July 1934.

HMS CARLISLE (21 August 1928)

The CARLISLE was one of the last group of the C Class cruisers, with five 6 inch guns, four twin torpedo tubes and a trawl bow. Completed by Fairfield in November 1918, she had served at Harwich for a short period and in 1919 sailed for the China Station. She left Singapore in July 1928 and is seen here entering Malta on her way to pay off at Sheerness. After a refit she served on the African Station for 8 years. She was converted to an AA ship at Chatham in 1939, with four twin 4 inch guns. She saw action in Norway in April 1940 and in May sailed for the Mediterranean. During the evacuation of Crete she was bombed and her Captain was killed. In 1942 she escorted Malta Convoys and was at the Second Battle of Sirte. She was at the invasion of Sicily and in October 1943 was badly damaged in the Aegean. She then became a base ship at Alexandria and was hulked there in 1948.

HMS CARYSFORT (28 February 1929)

The CARYSFORT was launched at Pembroke Dock on 14 November 1914. A CAROLINE Class cruiser, she is seen here sailing for the Far East on a trooping trip with relief crews for the gunboats, sloops and TITANIA. She returned to Devonport on 7 July after a five month round trip to China. She was the only one of the class fitted with Brown Curtis turbines, the remainder having Parsons independent reduction turbines. She joined the Reserve Fleet on returning to Devonport and was sold in August 1931.

HMS CENTAUR (1925)

CENTAUR and CONCORD were two cruisers built to use machinery and other materials originally destined for two Turkish ships. The last of the C class to have a clipper bow, they were designed to carry a uniform 6 inch gun armament, and had a fifth gun fitted between the bridge and funnels. By the time of this photograph, CENTAUR had had the extra gun replaced by a deckhouse. Their bridges were further forward to allow space for this gun, and CENTAUR was the first cruiser built with a tripod foremast. In April 1925 she commissioned at Portsmouth as the Flagship of Commodore Atlantic Fleet Destroyer Flotillas, who controlled 20 destroyers in full commission and 18 others in reserve or with reduced complements. In the 1930s the Kings of Sweden and Denmark hoisted their flags onboard as Honorary Admirals of the Fleet. She was placed in reserve in 1932 and sold in 1934.

HMS CENTURION (1928-9)

The CENTURION was a KING GEORGE V Class battleship, launched at Devonport in November 1911. She served at Jutland and in the Black Sea operations after the First World War. In 1927 she was converted to become a fleet target ship, being fired at by guns of up to 8 inch calibre. During firing she was controlled both for course and speed by radio messages sent from the destroyer SHIKARI, who would also embark CENTURION's steaming crew during the shooting. In 1928 she was at Malta from April to June, and in 1929 she was there from January to June. She also spent 5 months in the Mediterranean in 1930, 1931, 1934, 1935 and 1938. During the Second World War she was converted into a dummy (1939) KING GEORGE V Class battleship and served in the Mediterranean. She was converted again in 1944 to a blockship, and was sunk off Omaha Beach on 9 June 1944. The cruiser beyond is one of the CERES Class, probably the CURLEW.

HMS CERES (February 1929)

The CERES was the nameship of her class, being launched at Clydebank on 24 March 1917. In this class the bridge and boiler rooms were moved slightly aft, and the second 6 inch gun was mounted in a superfiring position forward of the bridge. This not only improved the firepower ahead, but gave a better weight distribution and improved the sea-keeping qualities of the class. She served with the Grand Fleet in the First World War, and afterwards in the Baltic. Here she is seen entering Grand Harbour from Volo prior to sailing for Marseilles to take the First Sea Lord to Pollensa Bay. Later in the year she relieved her sister, the CARDIFF, as Flagship of the Third Cruiser Squadron. In the Second World War she served in Home waters, then the Mediterranean and East Indies. She took part in the Normandy landings before becoming an accommodation ship. She was sold in July 1946.

HMS CHAMPION (July 1929)

The CHAMPION and her sister the CALLIOPE were built to test larger boilers and geared turbines. Having 6 boilers instead of the 8 carried in the previous C Class, they also introduced the two funnel arrangement. CHAMPION was fitted with two shafts, whilst CALLIOPE had four. She reached 29 knots on trials, leading to later C Class groups having only two shafts. Originally armed with two single 6 inch aft and eight 4 inch forward and abeam, by the time of this photograph her armament was a uniform four 6 inch guns. In 1928 she visited Reval to bring back the bodies of the crew of the submarine L55 from the Russians. In 1929 she was the Gunnery and Torpedo School cruiser, taking RNVR personnel on spring cruises. She was damaged by torpedoes in 1929 and 1931. In November 1933 she was relieved by the CURACOA and was sold in July 1934.

HMS CHRYSANTHEMUM (1921)

The CHRYSANTHEMUM is seen here entering Grand Harbour with a Battle Practice Target. She had been launched at Elswick on 10 November 1917 as a FLOWER Class sloop of the ANCHUSA Group. This group were designed to look like basic tramp steamers because of the success of early Q ships. She was fitted out for target towing in 1920 at Devonport, and also for fleet photography. She then served on the Mediterranean Station until May 1937, when she was converted to be a Drill Ship for the RNVR. She was berthed at the Embankment in April 1939 and remained there until sold to Inter London Action—a Children's Charity—in 1987.

HMS CLEOPATRA (February 1929)

Launched by Devonport Dockyard on 14 January 1915, the CLEOPATRA joined the Harwich Light Cruiser Squadron on completion and sank the German destroyer G194 by ramming in March 1916. In the same action she was damaged by colliding with the cruiser UNDAUNTED. Five months later she hit a British mine off the Dutch coast. After the war she took part in operations in the Baltic. During the war her original pole foremast was replaced by the tripod seen here. At this time she was on a trooping run to the China Station with the DARTMOUTH, reaching Shanghai in April and returning to Sheerness in June. She carried out a further trooping trip to Hong Kong in the autumn. She was sold in June 1931.

Commander-in-Chief's Barge (June 1929)

The 50 feet long steam picket boat is seen here in its most highly polished form as the barge of the Commander-in-Chief, Portsmouth, then Admiral Sir Roger J B Keyes Bt KCB KCVO CMG DSO LLD. There is a lifebuoy resting on a barricoe forward, whilst two ladies enjoy the trip in the shelter of a curtained cabin aft. Originally designed to be carried by battleships, these boats were able to mount a gun, and the earlier capital ships carried torpedoes for use by their larger boats.

HMS COMUS (1925-1928)

The COMUS was a CAROLINE Class cruiser, launched by Swan Hunter on 16 December 1914 and completed in May 1915. In this view taken at Portland whist she was serving with the Second Cruiser Squadron of the Atlantic Fleet, her final armament of 4 single 6 inch guns can be seen. Originally she carried two single 4 inch guns on the forecastle, which were replaced by a single 6 inch. She also had two single 4 inch on each side on the upper deck amidships, which were removed and a single 6 inch fitted abaft the funnels. Single 4 inch guns mounted abreast the foremast on each side were replaced by single 3 inch AA guns. She sank the raider GREIF in February 1916 and was at Jutland. She was paid off in March 1930 and was sold in July 1934.

HMS CONCORD (February 1927)

The CENTAUR and CONCORD were built by Armstrong using material and machinery intended for two Turkish ships that had been cancelled. They differed from previous C Class ships in having a uniform 6 inch armament, with a fifth gun placed between the bridge and funnels. For this, the bridge had been moved forward, and thus the ships were bow heavy. CONCORD saw active service in the 5th Light Cruiser Squadron based at Harwich from 1916-19, and then served in the Mediterranean until 1927 with breaks for a refit and also spells in Australian and Chinese waters. She is seen here with her full armament of 6 inch guns, and with 3 inch AA guns forward and aft of the searchlight control position. Later ships had the AA guns mounted athwartships to give better coverage. In August 1917 she was relieved by the CALEDON and was placed in reserve. She carried out trooping duties to China and worked with the Signal School before being sold in August 1935.

HMS CURACOA (11 September 1929)

One of the CERES Group of C Class cruisers, CURACOA was completed by Pembroke Dockyard on 18 February 1918. This was the first group with a second gun forward of the bridge, with the bridge and boiler rooms moved slightly aft. This made them better seaboats and improved their firepower on the forward arcs. She served as Flagship of the 5th Light Cruiser Squadron at Harwich in the First World War, but was mined in May 1919 just after she had become the Flagship in the Baltic. Here she is seen sailing for Malta from Portsmouth, having been refitted at Chatham. She was relieving the CARDIFF, who had been the 3rd Cruiser Squadron Flagship for 10 years. In 1940 she was converted to AA work, her 6 inch guns being replaced by four twin 4 inch guns and a quadruple pom pom. She was lost in a collision with RMS QUEEN MARY 20 miles NW of Bloody Foreland, Donegal, on 2 October 1942. 338 lives were lost.

HMS CYCLOPS (1928)

The CYCLOPS is seen here entering Grand Harbour. She was the Depot Ship for the First Submarine Flotilla, which she had brought out to Malta in December 1926. At that time the Flotilla comprised a mixture of vessels, X1, K26 and 5 L class submarines. CYCLOPS remained in the Mediterranean until 1938, when she was relieved by the MAIDSTONE, though she returned home for both Spithead reviews. Launched in 1905, she had been purchased whilst building and was used as a repair ship in the First World War. She was converted to a submarine depot ship in 1920. Here her sailors can be seen wearing pith helmets and her steam picket boats are stowed abaft the mainmast. She has a leadsman in the chains abreast the foremast. She served in home waters in the Second World War, paid off in 1945 and was sold in 1947.

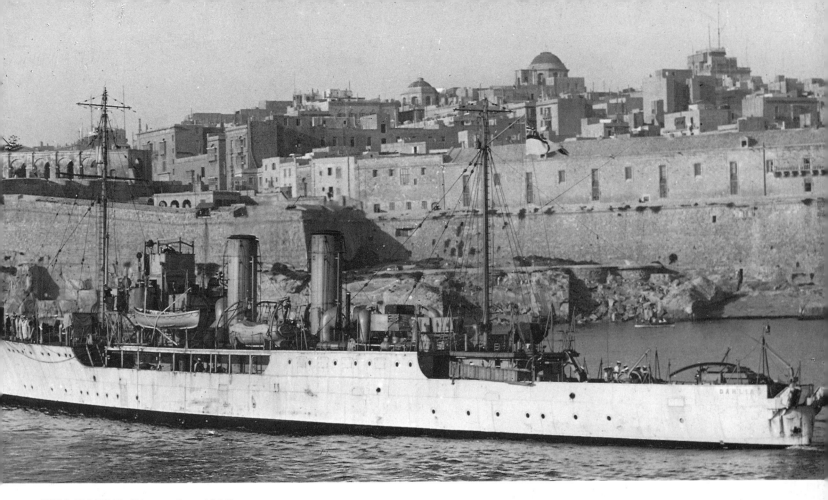

HMS DAHLIA (November 1926)

The DAHLIA was of the ACACIA Group of the FLOWER Class Sloops, which were designed for rapid construction during the First World War, with an average building time of 25 weeks. DAHLIA was launched by Barclay Curle in April 1915. In September of that year she was mined while minesweeping in the Cromarty Firth. These ships had a triple hull at the bow to strengthen them against mine damage. Of 1200 tons and with a speed of 16½ knots, they were very useful vessels and were employed in a wide variety of post war roles. DAHLIA was a temporary Reserve Drill Ship at Newport from 1923 to 1926. She commissioned at Chatham on 28 October 1926 and here is seen arriving at Malta to relieve the CORNFLOWER on Red Sea duties. DAHLIA was sold in July 1932.

HMS DANAE (19 February 1927)

The DANAE is seen here departing from Malta for the China Station, having had 48 hours to paint the ship's bottom, fuel, store and embark war outfits. She had commissioned for the First Cruiser Squadron in the Mediterranean in September 1925 and the whole Squadron, except for the DAUNTLESS, was sent out to China to deal with the crisis there. She returned to the Mediterranean in the December. At that time she was commanded by Captain B H Ramsay MVO, later famous for the evacuation of Dunkirk and the Normandy landings. She shared with the BARHAM the reputation of being the smartest ship on the station. The first D Class cruiser completed, she had no aircraft fit nor trawl bow. During the war she served mainly in the East, but in October 1944 became the Polish CONRAD until September 1946, when she was placed in reserve. She was sold in 1948.

HMS DARTMOUTH (June 1929)

The DARTMOUTH, a WEYMOUTH Class cruiser of 5250 tons, is seen here entering Portsmouth after a trooping voyage to the Mediterranean. Completed in October 1911 by Vickers, she was designed for 25 knots, but achieved almost a full knot more on trials. This class introduced a uniform armament of eight 6 inch guns. The tripod foremast and control top were fitted during the war. In 1914 she hunted German raiders, then in 1915 was at the Dardanelles. For the rest of the war she was in the Adriatic and was damaged by a torpedo from UC 25 on 15 May 1917. Her post war service was mainly in reserve and trooping duties. Temporarily attached to the DEFIANCE at Devonport in 1930, she was sold in December of that year.

HMS DAUNTLESS (October 1926)

The DAUNTLESS was a D Class cruiser, completed by Palmers in December 1918. She was armed with six 6 inch guns, twelve torpedo tubes and carried aircraft in a hangar under her bridge. The first member of the class to complete had no aircraft, DAUNTLESS and DRAGON had this hangar arrangement, whilst later units were fitted with a revolving flying off platform abaft the funnels. At this time DAUNTLESS was part of the First cruiser Squadron in the Mediterranean, and had just been to the Fleet Assembly at Volo in September, and then gone through the Dardanelles to visit Bergas (Bulgaria) and Constanta (Rumania). In July 1928 she ran aground off Halifax and was pulled off by her sister ship, the DESPATCH. During the war she served in the South Atlantic, China Station and Eastern Fleet before returning to Home Waters for training duties. She was sold in April 1946.

Picture Overleaf...DISCOVERY (May 1929)

The DISCOVERY was launched on 21 March 1901 by the Dundee SB Co, having been built specially for the first National Antarctic Expedition under the command of Captain R F Scott. She carried out two further voyages to the Antarctic between 1925 and 1927 and here she is seen prior to sailing on her last voyage to that area under the late Sir Douglas Mawson. She has her sails set and the funnel of her auxiliary engine is lowered. Her bow is almost solid timber sheathed with steel plates, and raked to allow her to ride up and crush ice underfoot. Her stern is rounded with an overhang to protect the rudder. A spare rudder was carried and the propeller could be lifted into a well. In 1931 she was laid up in the East India Dock and was later presented to the Boy Scouts and berthed on the Embankment. In 1955 she was taken into use by the Admiralty and carried the Flag of the Admiral Commanding Reserves from 1960-1976. In April 1979 she was handed over for preservation, and returned to Dundee in 1986.

HMS DIOMEDE (September 1928)

The DIOMEDE was launched by Vickers in April 1919, but was towed to Portsmouth for completion. She first commissioned in October 1922, and 3 years later became part of the New Zealand Division. She is seen here sailing from Portsmouth, after recommissioning, on her return voyage to Auckland via Gibraltar, Trinidad, Panama, Hawaii and Fiji. She reached Auckland on 17 November, six months after sailing for Portsmouth. Being a later member of the D Class, she had a trawl bow forward and a revolving flying off platform amidships. Her forward 6 inch gun was mounted in a gunhouse. After 10 years with The New Zealand Division she returned to the Royal Navy, serving in home waters and the South Atlantic in World War II, for a period as part of a USN Task Force. She became a Training Ship in 1942 and was sold in 1946.

HMS DOUGLAS (June 1929)

The DOUGLAS was a CAMPBELL Class destroyer leader, launched by Cammell Laird on 8 August 1918. At this time she was partly disarmed, B gun being replaced by a deckhouse and her after torpedo tubes landed whilst she acts as the leader of the First Submarine Flotilla in the Mediterranean. A leadsman can be seen working in the chains under the port bridge sponson as she leaves Portsmouth harbour. She became a short range escort in the war, her armament having been reduced to two 4.7 inch guns. She helped sink U732 on 31 October 1943 off Tangiers. She was sold in March 1945.

HMS DRAGON (August 1926)

The second ship of the D Class, the DRAGON was fitted with a hangar under her bridge and did not have a trawl bow. In August, 1918, on completion by Scotts, she joined the 5th LCS at Harwich. She is seen here as part of the 1st Cruiser Squadron in the Mediterranean, arriving at Malta from Argostoli and Trieste. In this view the single 6 inch guns forward and aft of her funnels can be seen together with the two starboard sets of triple torpedo tubes mounted on her upper deck. In 1927 she was temporarily detached to China and in 1928 was refitted, spending the next 9 years on the America and West Indies Station. During the war she served with the Home Fleet and in the Mediterranean, West Indies and South Atlantic. She was part of the ABDA Force off Singapore in January 1942 and reached Ceylon safely. She was manned by the Polish Navy from January 1943, was badly damaged by a torpedo off Normandy in June 1944 and was then used as a breakwater there.

HMS EAGLE (1928)

The EAGLE had been laid down as a Chilean battleship, the ALMIRANTE COCHRANE. She was completed as an aircraft carrier by Armstrongs in 1920, and after preliminary trials underwent alterations at Portsmouth untill April 1924. She had a speed of 24 Knots and was armed with nine 6 inch guns and carried 4 inch AA guns forward and aft of her island. She carried 21 aircraft and introduced the 'island' and a double storey hanger. In 1927 she assisted with the arrangments for the Schneider Trophy Cup taking place at Venice, and in 1928 provided aid at Corinth where an eartquake had made 10-15 thousand people homeless. During the war her aircraft were active in the Mediterranean and Red Sea, and she carried out nine ferry trips to Malta (delivering 183 aircraft) in 1942. She was sunk on the 11th August 1942 when torpedoed by U73 while escort'ng a convey to Malta.

HMS EMPEROR OF INDIA (July 1929)

The EMPEROR OF INDIA was laid down as the DELHI but was launched on 27 November 1913 at Vickers under her new name. An IRON DUKE Class battleship, she was in the Grand Fleet for the First World War—serving at Jutland. She then served with the Mediterranean Fleet for 7 years. She is seen here having just commissioned for the Atlantic Fleet as Flagship of the Third Battle Squadron. She transferred the Flag to her sister, the MARLBOROUGH, in January 1931 when she paid off. On 10 June 1931 she was used as a target and was sunk on the Outer Ower Shoal by the IRON DUKE. She was raised and taken to Portsmouth in August, being sold in December 1931 for scrap.

HMS ENDEAVOUR (November 1926)

A Survey Vessel of 1280 tons, launched by Fairfield on 30 March 1912, she was specially built for hydrographic duties. She had been surveying in the Red Sea in early 1926, then returned to Sheerness for a refit. After recommissioning on 15 October she sailed for the Red Sea again, and is seen here leaving Malta for the Suez Canal. In 1940 she became a depot ship, firstly at Singapore, then at Colombo. She was sold in September 1946.

FLYING BOAT S1125 (1926-8)

This Supermarine Southampton Flying Boat is seen taxi-ing outside Portland driven by its two Napier Lion engines. It had a top speed of 109 knots. Four of these aircraft made a flight from Felixstowe to Australia via Singapore starting in October 1927 and returning in 1928. The total journey was 23,000 miles with an average speed between stops of 65 knots. The RNAS and RFC merged into the RAF on 1 April 1918 and, it was not until 1 April 1924 that the shipborne element of the RAF was recognised as the Fleet Air Arm. Even so it did not come under complete control of the Admiralty until July 1937. Thus in the 1920s the RAF controlled the maritime elements of flying.

HMS FROBISHER (February 1929)

The FROBISHER was one of the Improved BIRMINGHAM Class cruisers. Their seven 7.5 inch guns had a 200 pound shell which was the heaviest that could be loaded by hand. Their engines were designed to be coal or oil burning, but FROBISHER was completed for oil only, enabling her to achieve 30½ knots. She was first commissioned in September 1924 at Devonport, 8 years after being laid down there. She sailed for the Mediterranean but in 1927 was sent to China where she helped destroy 40 pirate junks in March. In 1928 she recommissioned for the Mediterranean under Captain R B Davies VC DSO AFC, and was the Flagship of the First Cruiser Squadron. She was converted to a Cadets' Training Ship in 1932, two 7.5 inch guns being removed. She was re-armed for the war and served in the Eastern and Home Fleets. She was a bombarding ship at Normandy and was damaged by a torpedo in August 1944. After repairs, she again became a Cadets' Training Ship before being sold in 1949.

HMS FURIOUS (May 1929)

Originally built as a heavy cruiser and designed to carry two single 18 inch guns, the FURIOUS first had a hangar forward with a flight deck, and later, in November 1917, had the after turret replaced by a second hangar. Turbulence made the after flight deck dangerous and she was rebuilt in 1922-25. She is seen here in her full aircraft carrier guise, when her nickname had changed from 'The Spurious' to 'The Covered Wagon'. She was given a variety of improvements between the wars and later served with the Home and Mediterranean Fleets, covering convoys and carrying out ferry trips. She was laid up in 1945 and sold in March 1948.

HMS GLOWWORM (May 1928)

The INSECT Class River Gunboats were designed for working on the Danube but were called Chinese River Gunboats as a security cover. Many of the class did go to China. The GLOWWORM was employed on the defence of Lowestoft, then served in the White Sea before reaching the Danube in 1920. She displaced 645 tons, but drew only 4 feet. Armed with two six inch guns and a 3 inch AA gun she was manned by a crew of 60. She and MOTH were the only two of the class whose engines were oil fired. In 1921 Emperor Karl of Austria-Hungary abdicated and surrendered to the SNO Danube in the GLOWWORM, drafting and signing his own parole. After a summer cruise up the Danube in 1925 to Budapest and Vienna she was paid off in Malta. She was found to be damaged after she had gone to aid a burning ammunition ship and so was placed on the sales list in December 1927, and was sold to L Gatt of Malta in 1928. She is seen here disarmed, being towed out of Grand Harbour.

HM SUBMARINES H23 AND H34

The three submarines photographed here conducting manoeuvres at speed were of the improved H Class. The earlier H Class vessels had been built in Canada, the improved versions being built in Britain. They were slightly larger, at 434 tons displacement, and had four 21 torpedo tubes. H23 was launched by Vickers on 29 January 1918, and H34 on 5 November 1918 by Cammell Laird. The third vessel beyond is either H30 or H31. This photograph was probably taken between 1927 and 1929 when all three were serving with the training half of the Fifth Submarine Flotilla based at Gosport. Their depot ship was the ALECTO. They had a surface speed of 13 knots, and an underwater speed of 11.5 knots. H23 was sold in May 1934. H34 (one of three of the class with a straight top to her conning tower) served in the Second World War in home waters, and was broken up in July 1945.

HM Submarine H31 (July 1929)

H31 was launched by Vickers on 16 November 1918 and was completed on 21 February 1919. At the time of this photograph she was part of the training half of the Fifth Flotilla based at HMS DOLPHIN, with ALECTO as her depot ship. She is seen arriving off Portsmouth from exercises off Lamlash prior to sailing for a refit at Sheerness. She was part of the flotilla training anti-submarine vessels off Rothesay early in the war, but undertook war patrols off Brest when the German heavy surface units were there. She was lost on 24 December 1941 whilst on one of these patrols.

HM Submarine H33

H33 is seen here when part of the Sixth Submarine Flotilla based at Portland. She was launched by Cammell Laird on 24 August 1918 (one of three of the class with a flat top to her conning towers). She was with the Fifth Flotilla at Gosport when the war broke out, and then joined the training flotilla based on Rothesay. She undertook patrols off Brest in the spring of 1941 to watch for German heavy surface units. She was broken up at Troon in October 1944.

HM Submarine H50 (1926-29)

H50 was the last of her class to be launched (on 25 October 1919 by Beardmore). By this time some of the L Class, twice the tonnage and faster, were in service. H50 served with the Sixth Flotilla at Portland in the twenties, and during the war was with the training flotilla at Rothesay, giving anti-submarine training to escorts. She took part in war patrols in the spring of 1941—despite her age! She was sold and broken up in July 1945.

HMS HERMES (26 July 1924)

The HERMES was the first vessel specifically built as an aircraft carrier, having been launched by Armstrongs in September 1919 and completed, at Devonport, in August 1923. After trials she commissioned for the Atlantic Fleet. She is seen here at the first Spithead review of the Fleet after the war, with visitors onboard—together with RAF personnel on her flight deck. She had a hangar aft with an electrical lift from the quarterdeck to the flight deck. The hangar shutter door can be seen in this view. In the November she sailed for the Mediterranean and was diverted to the China Station, where she spent several commissions. During the war she served in the Atlantic and took part in the attack on Dakar in July 1940. She then sailed for the East Indies and took part in operations against the Italians in East Africa. She was sunk on 9 April 1942 by Japanese aircraft off Ceylon.

HMS HOOD (1925)

The battlecruiser HOOD was the only one of a class of four battlecruisers to be completed. She was launched on 22 August 1918 on the Clyde, and completed in March 1920. She displaced 41,200 tons and achieved just over 32 knots on trials. She was the last British capital ship with a control top, and with an open secondary battery. In 1923 she carried out a round the world cruise, covering 30,000 miles. Between the wars she was given refits to improve her AA armament. During the war she was employed on convoy escort duties and later joined Force H. In May 1941 she met the German battleship BISMARCK and was sunk. There were only 3 survivors.

HMS IRON DUKE (July 1929)

The battleship IRON DUKE is seen here just after commissioning in June 1929 as a seagoing gunnery firing ship, replacing the battlecruiser TIGER which had joined the Battle Cruiser Squadron whilst the HOOD was being refitted. She had been completed at Portsmouth in March 1914 and served with the Grand Fleet throughout the war, being Admiral Sir John Jellicoe's flagship at Jutland. This class were the last coal fired battleships and carried a main armament of ten 13.5 inch guns. Just after this commission she was 'demilitarised' to conform to the London Treaty, losing B and Y turrets and having her speed reduced to 18 knots. Used for training until 1939, she was stationed at Scapa Flow in 1939 to help defend the anchorage. She was near missed by bombs and settled on the bottom but continued in commission. She was sold in 1946.

HM Submarine K26

The K Class submarines were designed to operate with the fleet, having steam engines that could drive them on the surface at 23½ knots. When diving their funnels were lowered and watertight hatches placed over them. The residual steam in the engines was used when dived, and when that expired, their electric engines were started. K26 was launched at Vickers in August 1919 and was completed at Chatham in April 1923. She was of a slightly larger type than the earlier vessels, displacing 2140 tons and being 351½ feet long. She had three 4 inch guns, one can be seen forward of her conning tower and two were on the after structure. She had six bow and four beam torpedo tubes. Just after completion she sailed on a 20,000 mile cruise to the Far East —without a depot ship—and then joined the First Submarine Squadron. She is seen here at Malta, where she remained, being placed in reserve there in December 1930. She was sold to Namo Brothers Ltd, Malta in 1931.

HMS KENT (16 July 1928)

The KENT was in the first class of cruisers to be ordered after the First World War. She is seen here on passage to the China Station to take the flag of the Commander-in-Chief from the HAWKINS. She had been completed at Chatham on 25 June 1928, and is resplendent in her China Station colours. She served there until 1937, taking Admiral Sir Howard Kelly to Shanghai in January 1932, the first meeting between the Chinese and Japanese being held onboard. During her 1937 refit she, unlike her sisters, was not fitted with a hangar. She then returned to the China Station and spent the first part of the war in the East Indies. In 1940 she was in the Mediterranean and was damaged by a torpedo off Bardia and, during repairs at Devonport, was bombed. She then joined the Home Fleet, covering Russian convoys and raids on the Norwegian coast before being placed in reserve in 1945. She was sold in 1948.

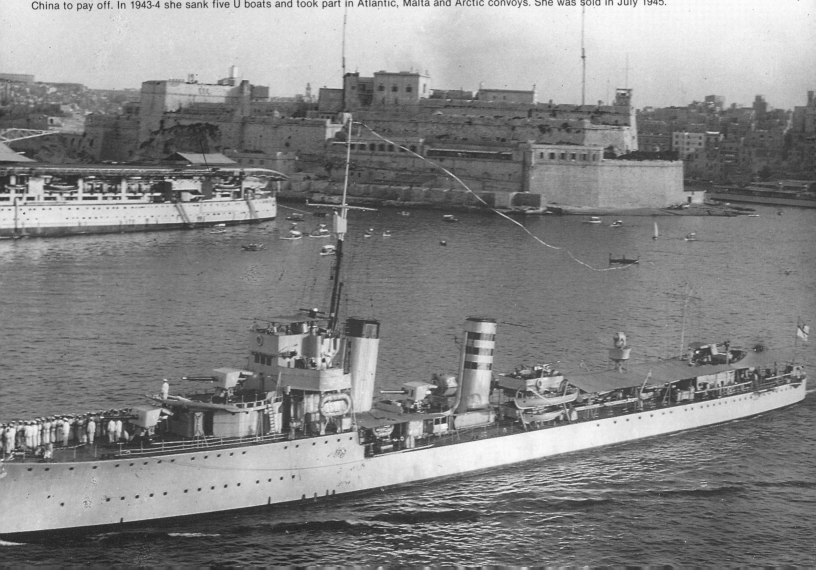

HMS KEPPEL (1928)

The KEPPEL was a Thornycroft Type destroyer leader launched on 23 April 1920 by Thornycroft and completed at Portsmouth in April 1925. Designed for 36 knots, the class did better on trials, one reaching 38.9 knots. She is seen here at Malta on her way back to Devonport from China to pay off. In 1943-4 she sank five U boats and took part in Atlantic, Malta and Arctic convoys. She was sold in July 1945.

HM Submarine L14 (25 June 1929)

The L Class submarines were an enlargement of the H class, being twice the tonnage. L14 was launched by Vickers on 10 June 1918, and was fitted to carry 16 mines. She had no gun and only four 21 inch torpedo tubes. When photographed she was serving with the Fifth Submarine Flotilla based at Gosport, and had been with the reserve half of the Flotilla under the PIGMY. She was placed in reserve in 1933, and was sold to Cashmore in May 1934.

HM Submarine L16 (May 1928)

L16 was launched by Fairfield on 9 April 1918 and was fitted with a single 4 inch gun and six 21 inch bow torpedo tubes. She is seen here entering Malta, with the Hospital ship MAINE and V and W Class destroyers in the background. She was part of the First Submarine Flotilla (under the depot ship CYCLOPS). Based in the Mediterranean from February 1927 to March 1931, she was sold in January 1934.

HM Submarine L19 (1929)

Launched on 4 February 1919 by Vickers, L19 was fitted with a 4 inch gun but had only four 21 inch bow torpedo tubes. She had been serving with the Fourth Flotilla on the China Station with the depot ship TITANIA and is seen here at Malta on her passage back to Sheerness to pay off. She had commissioned in China in November 1921 in lieu of L3, who had already been on station when the rest of the flotilla arrived. L19 was sold in 1937.

HM Submarine L21 (November 1927)

L21 is seen here at Malta, where she was serving as part of the First Submarine Flotilla with Captain SM1 in the CONQUEST. She had a single 4 inch gun and six bow torpedo tubes. At 238 feet long, this class was almost 70 feet longer than the H Class, and had a speed of 17 knots on the surface and 10½ knots submerged. L21 left the Mediterranean in 1931 and joined the Atlantic Fleet. She was sold in December 1938.

HM Submarine L25 (29 July 1929)

L25 was one of the L Class submarines fitted for minelaying. Launched by Vickers on 13 February 1919, she is seen here when operating as one of the experimental half of the Fifth Submarine Flotilla based on Gosport, under the depot ship ROSS. Earlier in the twenties she had operated with the Atlantic Fleet and also exercised in the Mediterranean. Here she is seen arriving at Gosport from Rosyth prior to sailing for Chatham. She was sold in October 1935 and was broken up at Newport.

HM Submarine L56 (1925)

L56 is seen here entering Msida Creek to go alongside her depot ship, the LUCIA. She was part of the Second Submarine Flotilla, comprising six of the L50 class submarines that had arrived in the Mediterranean on 8 May 1925, and remained there until 26 October 1926, when they sailed for Devonport. Originally armed with a four inch gun at each end of the conning tower, the after gun was replaced in 1925 by an ASDIC set. (See photo). This set (Type 113C) was fitted in four of the class and was the first in operational use by submarines. L56 had been launched by Fairfield on 29 May 1919 and displaced 960 tons. This class had 6 torpedo tubes and had a surface speed of 17.3 knots. She was sold in 1938 and was broken up at Pembroke Dock.

HMS LONDON (1929)

Nameship of the second group of the COUNTY Class cruisers, the LONDON is seen here just after completing at Portsmouth Dockyard on 31 January 1929. This group had internal hull protection, giving them an extra half knot over the first group, and their bridge and funnels were placed slightly further aft. Although designed to carry a catapult, manufacturing delays meant LONDON was without one for a short period. Shortly after working up and trials she sailed for the Mediterranean where she became the Flagship of the First Cruiser Squadron. She remained there till 1939 when she returned home for a major refit at Chatham, having a new bridge and superstructure on the lines of the COLONY Class. After an active war, she served in the Far East, being badly damaged trying to rescue the AMETHYST in 1949, when she lost 70 killed and 35 wounded. She was sold in 1950.

HMS LUCIA (1927)

The LUCIA is seen here with the Second Submarine Flotilla of L50 class submarines at Portland. They had returned to the Atlantic Fleet in December 1926 after two years in the Mediterranean. LUCIA had been built in 1907 as the Hamburg-Amerika liner SPREEWALD and was captured in September 1914 by the cruiser BERWICK. She was converted to a submarine depot ship in 1916 on the Clyde and served in the First World War on the Tees. In the Second World War she served in the East Indies, mainly at Colombo, being damaged there in April 1942 by Japanese aircraft. She was sold in 1946 and was broken up in 1951.

HM Submarine M2 (1928)

The M2 had been programmed as K19, one of the large steam driven submarines designed to operate with the fleet with a surface speed of 23½ knots. She was launched by Vickers on 19 October 1918 and was built with diesel/electric engines and fitted with a 12 inch gun taken from an old pre-DREADNOUGHT battleship. This gun would be loaded while the submarine was surfaced, but could be fired whilst the submarine was dived with the muzzle raised above the water. In 1924-27 she was again modified. The gun was removed and a hangar fitted forward. She could surface, fly off her aircraft and dive again within 5 minutes. Here she has her hangar doors closed, with a crane above the hangar and catapult ahead of it. She retained a single 3 inch gun aft. She was lost with all 70 officers and men off Portland on 26 January 1932.

HM Submarine M3 (1928)

M3 was one of the four K Class submarines that were altered to carry a single 12 inch gun, although M4 was not completed. M3 was originally K20 and was launched under her new number, on 19 October 1918, by Armstrongs. M3's 12 inch gun and after 3 inch gun were removed and, as can be seen, a mine rail was laid on top of her hull for two thirds of its length allowing her to carry 100 mines. The earlier L and K Class had had mine chutes in their ballast tanks. She commissioned in October 1928 and served in the experimental half of the Fifth Flotilla based on Gosport. She was sold in February 1932.

HMS MACKAY (1929)

The MACKAY is seen here entering Malta when leading the First Mediterranean Flotilla, which had originally been led by the MONTROSE. This view shows her triple torpedo tubes with the centre tube raised above the outer two. She had been launched as the CLAVERHOUSE at Cammell Lairds on 21 December 1918—her name was changed 10 days later. She became a short range escort during the war, landing three of her five 4.7 inch guns and being fitted with a twin 6 pounder in a large shield in A position. It had a rate of fire of 80 rounds per minute and was designed for use against E boats. She was sold in February 1947 and broken up in June that year.

RFA MAINE (1927)

The MAINE had been built as the PANAMA by Fairfield in 1902. She was purchased in 1920 and converted to a Hospital Ship, serving mainly in the Mediterranean. In February 1927 she passed through the Suez Canal for the China Station and was at Wei-Hai-Wei in July, and Hong Kong in October. She then sailed for the United Kingdom, arriving at Portsmouth on 17 December, before returning to the Mediterranean, arriving there in February 1928. In 1935 she was at Portsmouth again as a Government guest ship for the Silver Jubilee Review. Soon afterwards she was active in her proper role during the Spanish Civil War and later in the Second World War, when she had 13,000 patients. She was damaged at Alexandria in September 1941. In 1946 she helped with the casualties of the Corfu Incident. She paid off in 1947 and was sold in 1948.

HMS MALAYA (1929-31)

The MALAYA, a QUEEN ELIZABETH Class battle-ship, was a gift to Britain by the Federated Malay States. Completed four months before Jutland, she received 8 hits in that battle, losing 63 killed. She is seen here after her first big refit (1927-29) when her funnels were trunked and her bulges were fitted. The bulges and a flying off platform on B turret can be seen as she lies at Portland. In 1934 she was refitted again, a cross deck catapult and hangars being added together with an en-hanced AA armament. During the Second World War she was employed on convoy escort work (being torpedoed off Cape Verde in March 1941) and also undertook bombardments. Placed in care and maintenance in December 1943, she was later commissioned for bombarding duties at Normandy. Her latter years were spent as a train-ing ship before she was sold in February 1948.

HMS MARLBOROUGH (1927)

The MARLBOROUGH was completed on 16 June 1914 at Devonport Dockyard. She was Flagship of Vice Admiral Sir Cecil Burney KCB KCMG, Second in Command of the Grand Fleet at Jutland, where she was torpedoed and badly damaged. However, she managed to hold her position and did not transfer the Flag until the next day. In 1919 she sailed for the Mediterranean and was at Yalta in April embarking members of the escaping Russian Imperial family. In 1925 she and the other IRON DUKE class battleships reduced their complements to undertake boys' training. In August 1927 she relieved TIGER as Gunnery Firing Ship and in November carried out a trooping trip to the Mediterranean. In 1931 she paid off and was used for explosive tests in Plymouth Sound and needed docking before being taken to Portsmouth for use as an aircraft target in 1932. She was broken up in June 1932.

HMS MEDWAY (1929)

The MEDWAY was the first large submarine depot ship designed and built for the Royal Navy. She was launched at Barrow by Vickers Armstrong on 19 July 1928 and was commissioned at Devonport on 6 July 1929. She is seen here just after completion. She sailed for China with six of the recently completed O class submarines to replace the TITANIA and her L class submarines. She remained on the China Station until April 1940 when she was sent to the Mediterranean. On 30 June 1940 she was torpedoed by U372 off Alexandria whilst on passage to Haifa. 30 of her crew were lost, a Third Officer WRNS being mentioned in despatches. Fortunately 47 of her stock of 90 torpedoes floated clear but much valuable equipment was lost with her.

MINESWEEPING FLOTILLA (1927-29)

In this general view of Portland, with battleships and battlecruisers in the background together with cruisers and the depot ship ADAMANT, the focus is on the Auxiliary Patrol. In the foreground are 6 of the 7 Later HUNT Class minesweepers that made up the First Minesweeping Flotilla, with two MERSEY Class trawlers outboard of them. The MERSEY Class vessels were used for training RNR personnel in minesweeping, and these are either the BOYNE and CHERWELL or the GARY and LIFFEY. These vessels exchanged duties with the Fishery Protection gunboats. Beyond can be seen the Patrol Sloop PC74 outboard of an R Class destroyer, both probably working with the Anti-Submarine Flotilla.

HMS MONTROSE (May 1928)

The MONTROSE is seen here leaving Malta for Suda Bay and exercises. She was then leading the First Mediterranean Flotilla, before being relieved by the MACKAY in June 1929. Launched on 10 June 1918 by Hawthorn Leslie, she achieved 35.92 knots on trials and was completed in time to take part in operations to prevent German ships leaving Zeebrugge in October 1918. She became a short range escort in the Second World War, reducing her armament to two 4.7 inch guns but being fitted with a twin 6 pounder anti-E boat gun in A position. She was damaged in the evacuation of Dunkirk and destroyed an E boat off Yarmouth in February 1943. She also served on Atlantic and Arctic convoys and was at the Normandy landings. She was sold in January 1946.

HMS MOY (September 1926)

The MOY was a MERSEY Type trawler, built by Cochrane, and launched on 22 May 1917 as the ALEXANDER HILLS. She was renamed in 1920 and became part of the Fleet Target service in 1921, serving in the Mediterranean from then until the war. She is seen here entering Grand Harbour with a target alongside to port. During the war she remained in the Mediterranean until November 1944, being employed as a danlayer from 1943. She then returned to the United Kingdom. Laid up in 1946, she was sold in that November for commercial use, being renamed CORAL ISLAND.

HMS NELSON (1928)

The NELSON is seen here anchored in Portland Harbour wearing the flag of the Commander-in-Chief, Atlantic Fleet. She had been completed in June the previous year by Armstrongs, and was to wear the flags of seven successive Commanders-in-Chief. Her unusual looks were the result of designers trying to remain within inter-war treaty limits. Part of the weight saving involved placing the engine rooms forward of the boiler rooms. Her beam of 106 feet was sufficiently narrow to allow her to pass through the 110 feet wide Panama Canal locks. Her construction was strong enough for her to withstand being mined twice and torpedoed once during the Second World War. She served in Home and Mediterranean waters until D Day, then proceeded to the Far East, being at Singapore for the official surrender there. She became a training ship before being sold in 1949.

HMS ORMONDE (May 1929)

The ORMONDE was a '24' Class, or RACEHORSE Class, minesweeping sloop, launched by the Blyth Shipbuilding Co on 8 June 1918. This class had a single upright funnel with a bridge forward and aft and a single mast, which half the class had forward of the funnel, and half had abaft the funnel. Their 'push-me-pull-you' appearance made it hard for submarines to tell which way they were going. The ORMONDE was converted to a survey vessel at Devonport in 1923 and then served on the North America and West Indies Station. In February 1927 she recommissioned and spent the next two years off the Malayan coast and is seen here on her way back for a refit. She recommissioned in September 1929 for the Persian Gulf and in 1935 was surveying in the Mediterranean before paying off in that July. She was sold in August 1937.

HMS P40 (1928)

The P40 was a patrol boat launched by White on 12 July 1916. Of 613 tons these vessels were designed to carry two 4 inch guns and two torpedo tubes and steam at 23 knots. They had a low silhouette and were fitted with a hardened steel ram to attack submarines. Originally they had no weatherproof charthouse and were very wet. P40, seen here, has an enclosed bridge, only one four inch gun and her torpedo tubes had been replaced by depth charges. 48 of this class were built, but only three remained by 1928. P40 was sold in 1937 and was broken up at Milford Haven.

HMS PC74 (1927-9)

The PC Class of patrol sloops were P class patrol boats built up on the stocks to look like a tramp steamer and become decoy ships. Their 4 inch gun was concealed under a false deck cargo and they had 12 pounders by the charthouse. PC74 carried a 3 inch gun instead of a 12 pounder—it can be seen aft of her boat. She was launched by White on 4 October 1918, too late to operate in the First World War. Their plan of operation was to steam with a convoy in an outer position, and rely on their shallow draught (8 feet) to allow any torpedo to pass beneath them. Then they would use their high speed of 20 knots to attack the submarine. PC74 served as the decoy ship CHATSGROVE for the first month of the Second World War. She was sold in July 48.

HMS PANGBOURNE (1927-30)

Looking trim and smart off Portland is the PANGBOURNE, a Later HUNT Class minesweeping sloop. The wisp of smoke from her funnel belies the coal fired boilers, serving twin vertical triple expansion engines. These ships could achieve 16 knots, but needed best Welsh anthracite. The class became known as 'Smokey Joes' in the Second World War. PANGBOURNE had been launched by Lobnitz on 26 March 1918. Her total building time was under 8 months. 56 of the class were built, and completed just in time to undertake the task of clearing the minefields after the war. Most had paid off by 1927, but PANGBOURNE and 6 others formed the First Minesweeping Flotilla at Portland. She served throughout the Second World War and was sold for merchant service in March 1947.

HMS QUEEN ELIZABETH (14 May 1924)

The QUEEN ELIZABETH was completed in December 1914 at Portsmouth Dockyard. This class was the first to mount the 15 inch gun and to be oil fired, having a speed of 24 knots. On completion she went to the Mediterranean to calibrate her guns and became involved in the Dardanelles campaign. She was the Grand Fleet Flagship at the German surrender. She is seen here sailing from Portsmouth to Rosyth as flagship of the Commander-in-Chief Atlantic Fleet in her original guise, prior to her first refit (in 1926) when her funnels were trunked. In 1937 she started a second major refit at Portsmouth, but had to complete at Rosyth. New engines were fitted as well as a new AA armament. She went on to join the Mediterranean Fleet, where she was damaged by limpet mines at Alexandria in December 1941. Repaired, she joined the Home Fleet and then the Eastern Fleet. She returned home in July 45 and was sold in June 1948.

HM Submarine R4 (1927)

The R4 was one of a class of 12 vessels, 2 of which were cancelled. They were ahead of their time, being faster underwater (15 knots) than on the surface (9½ knots). They had a single screw with contra-rotating propellers and an advanced hull design. R4 was launched on 8 June 1918 at Chatham Dockyard and was one of the two of the class to survive after 1923. She operated from Portland in the Sixth Submarine Flotilla, and became known as 'The Slug'. She worked for the anti-submarine school, where her high underwater speed allowed her to avoid the slower A/S vessels. Her life was not uneventful however, for she ran aground off Exmouth in November 1926 and on the West side of Portland Bill in March 1927, and was in collision with the destroyer THRUSTER in March 1928. She was placed in reserve in 1933 and sold in May 1934.

HM Submarine R10 (1927)

R10 was launched by Armstrongs on 5 October 1918. Displacing 420 tons, she was only 163 feet long and carried six 18 inch torpedo tubes forward. Designed for anti-submarine work, these vessels were known as 'Little Arthurs'. She was commissioned to work with the Sixth Submarine Flotilla operating from Portland in 1923 and spent the next few years in the Channel area. In December 1927 it was announced that she was to be sold instead of H24. She paid off in March 1928 and was sold to Cashmore in February 1929.

HMS RENOWN (1929)

The RENOWN was built by Fairfields in 20 months, her design having been approved in 10 days. Good looking, with six 15 inch guns and a speed on trials of 32.68 knots, RENOWN's lack of armour appeared her Achilles heel. She is seen here at Portland wearing the Flag of the Rear Admiral Commanding the Battle Cruiser Squadron (Rear Admiral ADPR Pound CB). RENOWN was refitted in 1923-6 with bulges. In 1936, however, she underwent a major reconstruction and was given a vastly improved AA armament and new machinery. She had a very active and useful career in the Second World War, engaging the SCHARNHORST and GNEISENAU off Norway in April 1940, and being part of Force H in 1940-42. She paid off in 1945 and was sold in March 1948.

HMS REPULSE (1927-28)

Originally ordered as an R Class battleship (the RESISTANCE), the REPULSE was built at John Browns—in 19 months—to a lengthened battlecruiser design. She was completed in September 1916 and saw action in the Heligoland Bight in November 1917 when she hit the German cruiser KONIGSBERG with her 15 inch guns, causing a serious fire. In 1919 she was refitted and given a 9 inch belt of armour along her sides which then distinguished her from her sister, the RENOWN. She was again refitted in 1934-6 but not as extensively as her sister ship. During the war she undertook convoy escort work, was in the Norwegian campaign and took part in the search for the BISMARCK. Sent to the Far East in late 1941, when well overdue for a refit and updating of her armament, she was with the PRINCE OF WALES off Malaya on 10 December 1941. They were attacked by aircraft and after avoiding 16 torpedoes the REPULSE was hit by at least five and sank rapidly with the loss of 513 officers and men.

HMS RESOLUTION (February 1929)

The RESOLUTION was launched by Palmers on 14 January 1915. One of the REVENGE Class, designed for coal burning but converted to oil whilst building. At 22 knots they were slower than the QUEEN ELIZABETH Class. Their secondary armament of 6 inch guns was placed further aft, however, and was drier. In 1922 RESOLUTION was fitted with a funnel cap to help keep the bridge clear of fumes,the others of the class not being so fitted until 1938-9. She was bombed at Narvik in May 1940 and torpedoed at Dakar in September 1940. In 1942-3 she served in the Indian Ocean. In 1944 she became part of a training establishment and was sold in May 1948.

RESOLVE

The RESOLVE was an R Class tug launched by the Ayrshire DY Co, Irvine, on 30 July 1918. She was coal fired, with twin screws and a single rudder and could reach 14 knots. She and her sister the RETORT, unlike their sisters, had no forecastles. These vessels did not have a towing winch nor spring loaded towing hooks, and so the length of the tow had to be decided before sailing. Employed on Dockyard service, she was sold in September 1950.

HMS RESTLESS (July 1929)

The RESTLESS was an Admiralty R Class destroyer, launched by John Brown on 22 August 1916. This class could be distinguished from the M Class as they had their after 4 inch gun mounted on a bandstand. Their midship 4 inch was mounted between the second and third funnels. At this time the RESTLESS was running as a tender to HMS EXCELLENT, the Gunnery School at Portsmouth. She was handed over to Wards in November 1936 in part payment for the MAJESTIC, which became the CALEDONIA.

HMS REVENGE (May 1926)

The REVENGE was completed by Vickers in March 1916. At Jutland she fired 15 salvoes in the main action, and took the Flag of Vice Admiral Burney after MARLBOROUGH had been torpedoed. In June 1920 she was part of the force landing 8000 Greek troops at Panderma in the Turko-Greek War. She is seen here as Flagship of the Atlantic Fleet, a position she retained, until relieved by the Nelson, in October 1927. Never given a major modernisation, she was employed on convoy escort duties in the Second World War and in 1944 became part of a training establishment. She was sold in March 1949.

HMS RODNEY

The RODNEY was launched on 17 December 1925 by HRH Princess Mary, Viscountess Lascelles, at Cammell Laird. She commissioned for trials on 10 August 1927, and then for the Atlantic Fleet on 7 December 1927. She and her sister ship, the NELSON, were known as 'Cherry Tree' ships, as they were cut down by the Washington Treaty. Their three triple 16 inch gun turrets were grouped together to reduce the armoured belt and save weight. The after gun caused blast problems when trained astern and so the secondary armament of twelve 6 inch guns in twin turrets had to be placed right aft. RODNEY achieved 23.8 knots on trials. During the war she was damaged by a bomb off Norway in 1940, and scored the first hit on the BISMARCK in that ship's last action in May 1941. She supported Malta convoys, when her 16 inch guns were used in the AA role, and took part in the landings in North Africa and Normandy. She was sold in 1948.

HMS ROWENA (1926-29)

The ROWENA is seen here whilst operating as part of the Anti-Submarine Flotilla based at Portland. She relieved the RAIDER in this role in May 1926 and then spent most of her time at Portland with visits to Tobermory and Lamlash. This view shows clearly her three single 4 inch guns and two twin torpedo tube mountings. Fitted with two sets of geared turbines, she was designed for 36 knots. She paid off in 1935 and recommissioned for the Mediterranean. In the next year she paid off again and was handed over to Wards in 1937 in part payment for the MAJESTIC.

HMS ROYAL OAK (1927)

The ROYAL OAK is seen here arriving at Malta in October 1927 for a refit, with her sister the RAMILLIES beyond. In this view her very high bulges are clear, and flying off platforms can be seen on B and X turrets. She had been launched on 17 November 1914 at Devonport Dockyard and served with the Grand Fleet throughout the First World War. The bulges were her main modernisation between the wars, improving her protection and reducing her speed by only one third of a knot. On 14 October 1939 she was torpedoed by U47 whilst at anchor at Scapa Flow, being hit once by the first salvo and four times by the second. She sank in 10 minutes after the second attack, 786 officers and men being lost.

HMS ROYAL SOVEREIGN (26 July 1924)

The battleship ROYAL SOVEREIGN is seen here at the 1924 Spithead review with visitors embarked. Completed by Portsmouth in May 1916, she did not take part in the Jutland action. Part of the Atlantic Fleet in 1924 she had just received her low bulges, which reduced her speed of 22 knots only slightly. Her flying off platforms on B and X turrets can be seen. In 1937 she was fitted with a McTaggart catapult on her quarterdeck, but this was removed at the start of the war. She served on convoy escort duties and was at the action at Calabria in July 1940. She then went to the East Indies, being refitted at Philadelphia in 1943. Placed in care and maintenance in January 1944, she was transferred to the Russian Navy as the ARKHANGELSK in May 1944. Returned to the Royal Navy in February 1949, she was sold two months later.

HMS ST ISSEY (November 1926)

ST ISSEY was a SAINT Class Rescue Tug, built by Napier and Miller of Glasgow in 1918. 56 of this class were ordered, 18 being cancelled when the war ended. They were powered by steam reciprocating triple expansion engines driving a single screw at 12 knots. She could mount a 12 pounder gun, but at this time she was employed on target towing duties in the Mediterranean. In 1939 she was fitted with her gun and undertook patrol duties off Malta and in the Eastern Mediterranean. She was sunk by U617 off Benghazi on 28 December 1942.

SEAPLANE DOCKING LIGHTER (1928)

This vessel seems to be the forerunner of the modern off shore rig support vessels, with a working area aft and a bridge right forward. It would appear that she would dock down to take an aircraft and then the gantry cranes could plumb the engines on the wings. Some have described the vessel as a kite balloon ship. She flies the RAF ensign, a reminder that the Admiralty did not gain control of the Fleet Air Arm until July 1937, and did not take over any airfields until May 1939. Thus, for the 1920s, the RAF carried out the maintenance of all aircraft and was responsible for maritime air operations including those from Portland where this vessel is anchored.

HMS SHIKARI (1928)

The SHIKARI was an Admiralty S Class destroyer, launched by Doxford on 14 July 1919 but completed at Chatham in March 1924 as a control ship for the target ship AGAMEMNON. The wireless cabin between the funnels sent signals through the short lattice masts at A and Y positions to direct the battleship's course and speed. The AGAMEMNON was later replaced by the CENTURION. The canvas screen rigged at forecastle level under the bridge was to allow the galley fires to operate, as the downdraught at sea tended to put them out. Although not completed as a warship, in 1939 she was converted to an escort and fitted with guns, depth charges and radar. She rolled heavily whilst on Atlantic convoy duty. She took part in the evacuation of Dunkirk, being the last ship to leave the harbour. She was sold in November 1945. Beyond her can be seen the WRYNECK, which was lost off Greece in 1941.

HMS SHROPSHIRE (1929)

The SHROPSHIRE was one of the second group of the COUNTY Class cruisers armed with eight 8 inch guns and built for 32.25 knots. She was completed by Beardmore on 12 September 1929 and is seen here just before sailing for the First Cruiser Squadron in the Mediterranean. Remaining in the Mediterranean until 1939, she was not given a major refit before the war. She was part of a South Atlantic hunting group in October 1939 and captured the German merchant ship ADOLF LEONHARDT in December. She took part in the East African campaign in 1940-41 and in 1942 started a refit at Chatham. Completing in June 1943 she joined the Royal Australian Navy as a replacement for the CANBERRA. She then served in the Pacific, being present at the battle for Leyte in 1944 and at the surrender ceremony at Sagami Bay, Japan in August 1945. She was laid up in 1948 and was taken to Dalmuir for breaking up in January 1955.

HMS SUSSEX (April 1929)

The SUSSEX was completed by Hawthorn Leslie on 11 April 1928, and is seen here arriving at Portsmouth shortly after commissioning—with a Chatham crew—for the First Cruiser Squadron in the Mediterranean. She arrived on station on 14 May and spent the next ten years there with a break in 1934-6 when she went to Australia in an exchange with HMAS AUSTRALIA. The lack of bulges along the hull in this second group of the COUNTY Class can be seen here. During the first year of war she was very active, intercepting a blockade runner in December 1939 and travelling as far as the East Indies. In September 1940 she was bombed whilst in dock at Greenock and partly capsized. Repairs took two years. She then served in the Home and Eastern Fleets, sinking a German tanker and shooting down two kamikaze aircraft. Post war she served in the Far East, paid off in 1949, and was sold in 1950.

HMS TARA (June 1929)

Launched by Beardmore on 12 October 1918, the TARA was an Admiralty S Class destroyer of 905 tons. One of this class was built in 25 weeks. Originally armed with three 4 inch guns, her after gun was landed whilst she served on experimental duties with the Signal School at Portsmouth. She still retained her two twin 21 inch torpedo tubes amidships, and also two single 18 inch, one each side of the bridge. The smaller torpedo tubes carried a 'cold shot' 320 pound warhead. Most of the class completed after the war were not fitted with them, whilst all but four of the class landed theirs when the war was over. TARA was relieved by the STRONGBOW in 1931 and was sold that December.

HMS THUNDERER (1926)

The THUNDERER was an ORION Class battleship and the last warship built by the Thames Ironworks, being launched on 1 February 1911. The class re-introduced the 13.5 inch gun, and THUNDERER carried out comparative trials using the Percy Scott director system with her sister, the ORION, which was not so fitted. THUNDERER scored six times as many hits despite ORION being the best gunnery ship in the Fleet at the time. In this class all the main armament was on the centreline. She was present at Jutland and after the war became a seagoing training ship for cadets. She is seen here paying off on completion of that duty. The last of her class and looking old fashioned with her foremast abaft the forefunnel. She was sold in December 1926 and arrived off Blyth for breaking up on Christmas Eve that year.

HMS TIGER (1928)

The battlecruiser TIGER is seen here at Portland while serving as the Gunnery Firing Ship. Launched on the Clyde in December 1913, she was an improvement on the LION Class, having a secondary armament of 6 inch guns and her main armament was laid out to give better arcs of fire. She served with the Grand Fleet in the war and was at Jutland where she received turret and side damage. Later her foretop was enlarged and an unsightly topmast was added aft. Flying off platforms were also added and one can be seen on B turret. She was relieved by the MARLBOROUGH in 1929 so that she could rejoin the Battlecruiser Squadron whilst the HOOD was refitting. She paid off in 1931, being the last coal fired capital ship in the British Fleet. She was sold in 1932.

HMS UMPIRE (1928)

An Admiralty Modified R Class destroyer of 1085 tons, this class had the bridge fitted further aft to improve seakeeping qualities, and the forward two funnels were trunked into one. She was launched by Doxford on 9 June 1917 and served in the North Sea during the War, being one of the screening destroyers during the Battle of Heligoland Bight in November 1917. She became a tender to HMS VERNON at Portsmouth in 1920 and in 1927 was one of the Portsmouth Emergency destroyers. She is seen here operating off Portland whilst on this duty. She was relieved by the TILBURY in April 1929 and was sold in January 1930.

HMS URCHIN (September 1928)

The URCHIN was launched by Palmers in June 1917 and served in the North Sea during the War. In the Battle of Heligoland Bight in November 1917 she was part of the screen for the COURAGEOUS and GLORIOUS. In 1927 she became one of the Portsmouth Emergency destroyers and was relieved in March 1929 by the TRIBUNE. A Modified Admiralty R Class destroyer, her 4 inch guns had an increased elevation to improve their range. She was sold in January 1930.

HMS VALIANT (1926)

The VALIANT was completed by Fairfields in February 1916, and joined the Fifth Battle Squadron. At Jutland she was the only ship of the Squadron to come out of Windy Corner unscathed. She is seen here before her first major refit (1929-30). The bulges in her side below her after turrets were for 6 inch guns, but the positions were too wet at sea, and so the guns were not fitted. She had a second major refit in 1937-39, and then carried out convoy escort work before joining the Mediterranean Fleet. She took part in bombardments and was at Matapan and Crete before being damaged by limpet mines at Alexandria in December 1941. After repairs she served in the Eastern Fleet with a spell in the Mediterranean. She was damaged when in a floating dock, which collapsed, at Trincomalee in August 1944. She returned to the UK and was sold in August 1948.

HMS VAMPIRE (12 December 1926)

The VAMPIRE was originally laid down at White's as the WALLACE, one of a class of five leaders. However, more vessels of the same type, but without the leader facilities were ordered to counter the threat from heavy German destroyers, and the V Class was formed. Completed in September 1917, she is seen here leaving Malta on paying off after 2½ years service in the Fifth Flotilla. By the summer of 1927 she was back in the Mediterranean in the First Flotilla. In 1933 she was transferred to the Royal Australian Navy, arriving at Port Darwin on 7 December 1933. She spent the first two years of the war in the Mediterranean and then underwent a six month refit at Singapore. In December 1941 she was with Force Z and rescued survivors from the REPULSE and PRINCE OF WALES. In January 1942 she left Singapore for Colombo and on 9 April was attacked by Japanese aircraft in the Bay of Bengal and sunk.

HMS VANOC (May 1929)

The VANOC was one of the Admiralty V Class destroyers, launched by John Brown on 14 June 1917. She is seen here leaving Portsmouth for Greenock to carry out torpedo trials. She could be converted for minelaying by the removal of her after tubes and gun. In the First World War she laid 965 mines. In the Second World War she assisted with the evacuation at St Nazaire in June 1940, and on 17 March 1941 rammed and sank U100 (Schepke), and whilst she lay stopped, the WALKER guarding her found and sank U99 (Kretschmer). She was converted to a Long Range Escort in 1943, and sank U392 in March 1944. She was sold in July 1945, being stranded at Penrhyn on her way to the breakers.

HMS VANQUISHER (July 1927)

The VANQUISHER was one of the Admiralty V Class which introduced superfiring guns to destroyer design. Launched by John Brown on 18 August 1917, she was armed with four 4 inch guns and two pairs of torpedo tubes. The torpedo tubes were replaced by triple mountings before this picture was taken. She took part in the Battle of the Heligoland Bight in November 1917, and in the Second World War helped at the evacuation of Dunkirk and St Nazaire. She was converted to be a long range escort in April, 1943, with her forefunnel removed, gunnery armament reduced and fitted with radar and extra depth charges. On 10 April 1945 she helped sink U878 whilst on convoy duty South of Ireland. She was sold in March 1947 and was taken to Charlestown for breaking up in December 1948.

HMS VANSITTART (August 1926)

The VANSITTART was a Modified W Class destroyer, launched by Beardmore on 17 April 1919. This class were fitted with four 4.7 inch guns and were built with two triple torpedo tubes. On trials VANSITTART achieved 37.09 knots, though designed for only 34. She is seen here as part of the Fourth Mediterranean Flotilla, having commissioned at Devonport on 29 April. In June 1942 she rescued the crew of the WILD SWAN, a half sister, which had been sunk in the Bay of Biscay after shooting down 6 of 9 attacking aircraft. VANSITTART was converted to a long range escort in June 1943 and was sold in February 1946.

HMS VEGA (July 1927)

The VEGA was an Admiralty V Class destroyer, launched by Doxford on 1 September 1917. Built with four 4 inch guns and two twin torpedo tubes, after the First War the twin tubes were replaced by triple mountings, which were lighter. She is seen here having just returned to the Mediterranean after recommissioning for the Second Destroyer Flotilla. In November 1939 she underwent a WAIR conversion at Devonport, when she was fitted with twin 4 inch guns at A and X positions, and given a new bridge. She was sold in March 1947 and broken up a year later.

HMS VENDETTA (1926)

The VENDETTA was launched by Fairfield on 3 September 1917. She served with the Grand Fleet during the First World War and was present at the Battle of Heligoland Bight in November 1917. In December 1918, in the Baltic, she was involved in the capture of Bolshevik destroyers. She is seen here leaving Malta on 12 December to pay off at Portsmouth after a commission under Lt Cdr W N T Beckett MVO DSO in the First Mediterranean Flotilla. During this commission she was visited by the King and some of the Royal Family who signed their names in paint on the Captain's cabin bulkhead. He later had the piece of bulkhead removed and hung in his home. VENDETTA was transferred to the Australians in October 1933. She was present at the Battle of Matapan and took part in the supply run to Tobruk. She was scuttled off Sydney Heads in July 1948.

HMS VENTUROUS (July 1927)

Launched by Denny on 21 September 1917, the VENTUROUS is seen here entering Malta having replaced the VENETIA in the Second Destroyer Flotilla. VENETIA required retubing, and VENTUROUS commissioned at Port Edgar in May 1927. She paid off at Devonport after 10 months in the Mediterranean. Smart looking and with a good armament, these ships were limited in endurance, having no refrigerator they relied on the local purchase of bread and food from ashore. She was handed over to Wards in August 1936 in part payment for the MAJESTIC.

HMS VISCOUNT (1927)

Launched on 29 December 1917, the VISCOUNT was a 'Thornycroft V' Class destroyer, differing from her half sisters in that she had a taller, flat sided after funnel. She had 3000 more shaft horse power to give her an extra knot, but she ran her trials at 37.8 knots, almost 4 knots faster than the other vessels. Here seen when with the Second Destroyer Flotilla in the Mediterranean, she was converted into a long range escort in December 1941. She sank U619 on 15 October 1942 and U69 on 17 February 1943, both whilst on Atlantic convoy escort duties. She was sold in March 1945.

HMS VIVACIOUS (February 1929)

The VIVACIOUS is seen here at Malta with a pair of light gunnery targets alongside. She was part of the First Flotilla in the Mediterranean, having commissioned in January 1927. Launched by Yarrows on 13 November 1917, her twin propellers were driven by Brown Curtis turbines. This class had a limited endurance for provisions, and also in fuel, their range, at 15 knots, being only 2600 miles. In February 1942 she was one of the destroyers that tried to stop the German heavy ships running up the Channel from Brest. Later that year she was converted to a long range escort. She was an escort for the follow up waves for the Normandy invasion and in May 1945 was in the force that entered Bergen. She was sold in March 1947 and was broken up at Charlestown in 1948.

HMS VULCAN (1928-30)

Originally built as a Torpedo Boat carrier, being launched at Portsmouth on 13 June 1889, the VULCAN was converted to a submarine depot ship in 1915. She is seen here in that role at Portland supporting the Sixth Flotilla comprising H class submarines and the R4. Shortly afterwards she was relieved by the TITANIA, which had just returned from the China Station. She then started a third career, being converted at Devonport prior to becoming DEFIANCE III, part of the Torpedo and Electrical School at Wilcove. She remained there until December 1955, when she was towed to Belgium for breaking up.

HMS WAKEFUL (May 1929)

The WAKEFUL was completed by John Brown on 20 November 1917 and undertook convoy and patrol duties in the First World War. In 1918 she served in the Baltic operations before becoming a tender at Devonport. She spent most of the 30s in reserve. At the time of this photograph she had just commissioned at Rosyth for the 6th Destroyer Flotilla of the Atlantic Fleet, with the crew of the WESTMINSTER. WAKEFUL's crew had commissioned the WOLFHOUND for trials a month before. At the start of the Second World War she was working in the Western Approaches. When the Dunkirk operations started she carried 639 troops home. She was torpedoed by an E boat on her second trip whilst steaming at 20 knots, and sank quickly with the loss of about 740 people, only 40 soldiers and 10 naval personnel being rescued.

HMS WANDERER (1929)

The WANDERER was a Modified W Class destroyer, having four 4.7 inch guns whose shells weighed 45 pounds compared to the 32 pounds of the 4 inch shell. Launched by Fairfields in May 1919, she spent most of the '20s in the Mediterranean, with a short period in China in 1927-8, and visits to Sheerness to recommission. When relieved by the ANTHONY in 1930, she was placed in reserve. In 1941 she helped sink U147 and U401 off Ireland. She was then converted to a long range escort and took part in the invasion of Sicily. In 1943 she helped sink U523 in the Bay of Biscay and in the next year U305 off Ireland. Whilst part of the Normandy landing escort force she helped sink U390 in the English Channel. She was sold in January 1946.

HMS WARSPITE (September 1928)

The WARSPITE was launched at Devonport on 26 November 1913. She was badly damaged at Jutland. She was the first of the class given a large refit and is seen here soon afterwards. She had just returned from the Mediterranean having struck an uncharted obstruction and flooded three double bottom compartments. She had a second major refit in 1934-37, being fitted with a new bridge structure, new machinery, and an improved main and AA armament. She took part in the Norwegian campaign, being at the Second Battle of Narvik. She joined the Mediterranean Fleet and was at Matapan and then was badly damaged at Crete. Repaired in America, she served in the Eastern and Mediterranean Fleets before returning home for the Normandy landings. She was sold in 1947, running aground in Prussia Cove on her way to the breakers and was broken up on site.

HMS WESTMINSTER (1929)

The WESTMINSTER was an Admiralty W Class destroyer completed by Scotts in 1918. She served in the Baltic in late 1918 and brought home the survivors from the mined cruiser CASSANDRA before joining the Atlantic Fleet. She is seen here returning from the Atlantic Fleet spring cruise looking smart but with boiler tube defects. She was relieved by the VIVIEN, and her crew commissioned the WAKEFUL. She was one of the first destroyers fitted with ASDIC. In January 1940 she underwent a WAIR conversion but in May that year was bombed off the Dutch coast and had to be towed to Chatham. She was employed on East coast escort work and was sold in March 1947.

HMS WHIRLWIND (1929)

The WHIRLWIND, an Admiralty W Class destroyer, was completed by Swan Hunter on 28 March 1918 and took part in the raids on Zeebrugge and Ostend. In the latter raid she towed her sister ship WARWICK which had been mined. She was one of the class fitted for minelaying and is seen here, partly disarmed, sailing from Portsmouth for a mining exercise off Portland. She was torpedoed by U34 SW of Ireland on 5 July 1940 and was lost.

HMS WINCHELSEA (1929)

Launched by Whites on 15 December 1917, the WINCHELSEA is seen here sailing from Portsmouth to join the Second Destroyer Flotilla in the Mediterranean. She spent the Second World War in Home waters. She was at Dunkirk, where she recovered almost 5000 troops. She was later praised by the C-in-C Western Approaches for her tow of the LEEDS CITY in January 1941. In April 1942 she was converted to a long range escort, with her forward funnel and boilers removed and speed reduced to 24 knots. She paid off in November 1944 and was sold in March 1945.

HMS WINCHESTER (1929)

The WINCHESTER, an Admiralty W Class destroyer of 1100 tons, was launched by Whites on 1 February 1918. At the time of this photograph she was part of the VERNON Flotilla and running from Portsmouth, having been recommissioned with the crew of the STRONGHOLD in January 1927. She was refitted to become a WAIR escort destroyer in April 1940, and on 15 May 1940 was damaged by bombs whilst trying to protect a Scheldt ferry off the Dutch coast. In March 1941, whilst at Woolwich, she was again bombed, and a near miss delayed the refit she was undergoing. She became an accommodation ship in August 1944 and was sold in March 1946.

HMS WISHART (1929)

The WISHART was a Thornycroft built vessel of the third group of Modified W Class destroyers. The two vessels of this group were unusual in having a large forefunnel and a tall after funnel, and they had no platform for an AA gun abaft the after funnel. She was launched on 18 July 1919 and completed in June 1920. She had served on the China Station and then in the Mediterranean. In the 1930s Lord Mountbatten was her Commanding Officer. During the war she had minor alterations and was used as a short range escort. She sank the Italian submarine GLAUCO in June 41 West of Gibraltar; helped sink U74 in the Western Mediterranean (in May 1942) and U761 (in February 1944) also near Gibraltar. She was placed in reserve in September 1944 and was sold in March 1945.

HMS WITCH (1929)

A Thornycroft Modified W Class destroyer, the WITCH was distinguishable by her large forefunnel and tall after funnel. Launched by Thornycroft on 11 November 1919, she was completed by Devonport on 31 March 1924 and then served in the Mediterranean during the '20s. Her badge was a black cat on a silver moon! She served on the China Station from 1932 to 1935 and during the war was in the Atlantic, being in Canadian waters in 1942. She refitted in New York in November 1942. In 1943 she operated off West Africa. She became a target ship in 1945 and was the last 'V and W' in commission in June 1946. She was sold in July 1946.

HMS WOLSEY (1929)

The WOLSEY was one of two Thornycroft W Class destroyers. As with all the Thornycroft V and W Class variations, she had 3000 more shaft horse power giving her an additional knot in speed. WOLSEY was the fastest of the V and W Classes, achieving 38.2 knots on trials. At the time of this photograph she was in the Mediterranean, having been out to China in 1926 and being brought back in 1927 by the crew of the WANDERER. In 1932-3 she was the temporary leader of the First Submarine Flotilla in the Mediterranean. In December 1939 she was converted to a WAIR escort vessel, with a new bridge, and twin 4 inch guns in A and X positions. She was damaged during operations off Dunkirk in May 1940 during which she recovered over 3000 troops and five years later was in the force that entered Stavanger. She was sold in March 1947, her twin 4 inch guns being fitted in a BAY Class frigate.

HMS WOLVERINE (27 August 1928)

Launched by Whites on 17 July 1919, the WOLVERINE was one of the second group of Modified W Class destroyers, with their two single 2 pounder pom poms fitted between their funnels. Their forefunnel was wider than the other groups, with the after funnel being thinner. She is seen here leaving Malta to pay off after a commission with the Third Flotilla in China. After recommissioning at Devonport she returned to the Mediterranean until 1930 when she was relieved by the ACASTA. She was then placed in reserve at Rosyth. She sank U47, which had sunk the ROYAL OAK in Scapa Flow, in March 1941. In the next month she helped sink U76. In August 1942 she was screening the aircraft carrier FURIOUS when she rammed and sank the Italian submarine DAGABUR off Algiers. She was painted a camouflage pink at one time, and became known as the 'Barmaid's Blush'. She was sold in January 1946.

HM Submarine X1 (December 1927)

The X1 was a cruiser submarine of 2780 tons, the largest RN submarine before the introduction of nuclear powered vessels. She was launched at Chatham on 16 June 1923 and was armed with two twin 5.2 inch guns and six torpedo tubes. Trials started in January 1924, but she did not commission fully until 1925. She was part of the First Flotilla in the Mediterranean and is seen here sailing from Malta after a short refit. Her main diesels could propel her at 19½ knots, but she could reach 26 with electrical overdrive. She suffered explosions in 1929 and 1931, and was then laid up. In 1936 she was given to Wards in part exchange for the MAJESTIC.

HMS YARMOUTH (June 1927)

Completed in April, 1912, by London and Glasgow, the YARMOUTH was a WEYMOUTH Class cruiser, carrying a uniform armament of eight six inch guns and designed for 25½ knots. YARMOUTH had two propeller shafts whilst the others of her class had four. She took part in the hunt for the EMDEM and then joined the Grand Fleet, being present at Jutland. In 1917 she was refitted with a tripod foremast. After the war she was placed in reserve and was attached to the Portsmouth Signal School. She was also used for trooping, and in February 1927 set out for the China Station with ratings and spare gun barrels for the gunboats there. On 15 March she damaged her starboard turbine and had to make for Colombo, where she was repaired. She is seen here returning home. Never fully repaired, and limited to 10 knots, she carried out experiments with the Signal School and carried the Flag of Rear Admiral (Submarines) before being sold in July 1929.

INDEX